WILD YET TASTY

A Guide to Edible Plants of Eastern Kentucky

SECOND EDITION

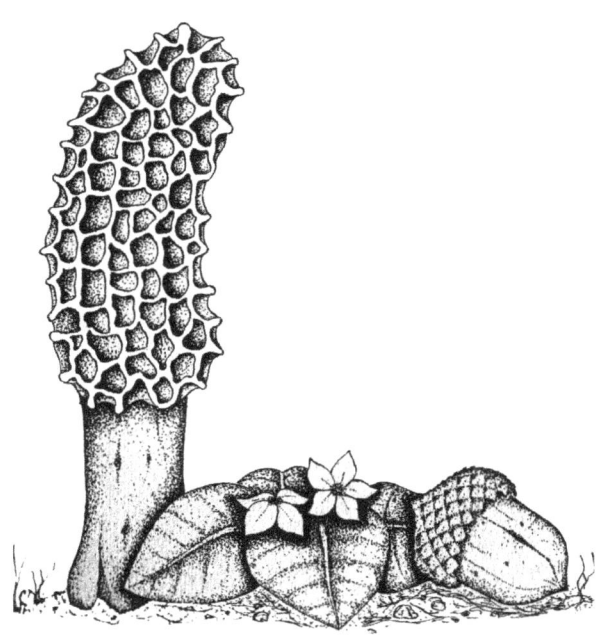

Dan Dourson
Judy Dourson

south limestone

Published by South Limestone Books
An imprint of the University Press of Kentucky

Copyright © 2019 by The University Press of Kentucky
All rights reserved

Editorial and Sales Offices: The University Press of Kentucky
663 South Limestone Street, Lexington, Kentucky 40508-4008
www.kentuckypress.com

NOTE OF CAUTION

The identification and consumption of wild edible plants should be done with caution. If you have identified an edible species, PRIOR TO CONSUMING re-check the illustration, identification, and habitat several times. Compare your findings with other references on the same species (see references in back for more information). If you are in doubt, DO NOT CONSUME the plant until you have personally checked with a qualified authority. If you do consume a plant for the first time, try only a small amount. This allows for individual variation in response to food (as with even our modern grocery store products) and is a safeguard in the event you misidentified the plant. Avoid collection of plants located immediately surrounding highways and areas that have been sprayed, for they will likely contain harmful chemicals. In other words, be more familiar with the species than you are with your own name!

Disclaimer: The authors and publisher shall not be legally responsible for the misidentification and ingestion of wild plants. All harvesting and consumption of wild plants is at your own risk.

The book is a revised version of the original *Wild Yet Tasty*, written and published originally in 1984 by Daniel C. Dourson.

ISBN 978-1-94-966903-9 (pbk : alk. paper)
ISBN 978-1-94-966905-3 (epub)
ISBN 978-1-94-966904-6 (pdf)

This book is printed on acid-free paper meeting
the requirements of the American National Standard
for Permanence in Paper for Printed Library Materials.

Manufactured in the United States of America.

TABLE OF CONTENTS

Introduction 1
Pictorial Description of Terms 5
Wild Edible Plants of Eastern Kentucky 8
    Common Greenbrier 9
    Redbud 10
    Toothwort 11
    Dandelion 12
    Partridgeberry 13
    Serviceberry 14
    Blackberry 15
    Blueberry & Huckleberry 16
    Wild Strawberry 17
    Wintergreen 18
    Sumac 19
    Persimmon 21
    Pawpaw 22
    American Beech 23
    American Chestnut 24
    Shagbark Hickory 25
    White Oak 26
    American Hazelnut 27
    Common Cattail 28
    Indian Cucumber Root 29
    Pine 30
    Common Morel 31
    Preparing Wild Foods 33
    Glossary of Terms 34
    References 35
    About the Authors 36

INTRODUCTION

In 1978-1979, I worked for the US Forest Service in Red River Gorge on a timber crew and later in the 1990s as the district's wildlife biologist. During this time, I learned of the numerous wild edibles. Early experiences came from the knowledgeable people with whom I worked, and later, my own research. One plant I shall never forget is the Indian turnip, or "jack-in-the-pulpit". While out marking timber one day (in the 1970's), my two co-workers, Wallace Booth and Roscoe Miller offered the corm of this interesting plant to taste. Being from the city and anxious to try anything new, I did not hesitate to sample.

While the first few bites are rather bland, what follows is nothing less than fire in the hole! As my two co-workers struggled to hide their hangdog grins, I thought, "What's so funny?" Than it hit me and my opinion of Wallace and Roscoe went from good old boys to those merciless bastards. Needle-like calcium oxalate crystals were flooding my mucus-membranes. Unable to speak coherently and give my co-workers a proper tongue-lashing, I had suffered my first uninformed encounter with a wild edible plant. The awful sensation lasted almost as long as their hearty laughter. I had just received a "bonafide city-slicker initiation"—a common practice here in eastern Kentucky. It never seemed all that funny until my brother John, daughter Angie, wife, Judy and sons, Brad and Tyler, Mark Gumbert and Brainerd Palmer-Ball, all somehow experienced similar mouth-burning encounters. Some say pay it forward. My family and friends say "Don't eat anything Dan pulls from the ground!" Believe or not Indian turnip is edible but only after the corms are thoroughly dried.

This unpleasant ordeal not only left a very bad taste in my mouth but also brings up an important caution regarding wild edible plants. <u>If this field of study is new to you, I strongly recommend that you read carefully the descriptions and pay close attention to the illustrations. It would also be wise to have at least one other resource book available as a cross-reference. Peterson's *A Field Guide to Edible Wild Plants of Eastern and Central North America* is highly recommended. Together, these manuals will greatly decrease the chances for misidentification.</u>

Wild Yet Tasty (A guide to common wild edible plants) follows a simple framework: a brief pictorial description of basic terms used for edible plants; a detailed illustration and description for each species is included as well as edible parts of the plant. In some cases, the entire species is drawn for further detail whereas others are only partially depicted. The description consists of four parts: NAME: common and locally-used names underlined with the scientific name in parentheses below IDENTIFICATION AND HABITAT: species characteristics and preferred location EDIBLE PARTS: specifics about edible plant parts BEST TIME TO HARVEST. GLOSSARY OF TERMS used throughout the book is found on page 34.

Learning to identify wild edible plants is as interesting as it is useful in times of emergency. But there are additional benefits to consider. Foraging for wild foods is an excellent way to slow down a frequently fast-paced life to nature's unhurried existence. For obvious reasons, this area of study merits both time and patience to identify each plant correctly. Slowing down our hurried pace allows our senses to fill with the sights, sounds and smells of our immediate surroundings, realigning ourselves with the natural world. The result? A rekindling of that sense of wonder we all had as kids. Perhaps this is by far the greatest value.

Environmental Message from the Authors
For a moment, imagine the ride of a lifetime, full of mystery and adventure around every turn. Throughout the ride you discover treasures beyond your wildest dreams. Bursting with excitement, your senses are on overload and best of all, it's free. The ride? Spaceship Earth, a wonderfully time-crafted vessel of unimaginable beauty hanging in the balance. The treasures discovered: life itself amid deep blue oceans and distant mountains shrouded in mist, teeming with a rich tapestry of plants and animals. But this scenario is silently and rapidly slipping away. Given the state of the environment, I often ponder the future of the planet and the quandary of our species. What were once pristine rivers of vitality are now gutters of spoil, oceans of prosperity turned to waters of poverty and forests untainted by human activities are becoming but distant memories. Our world is not infinite but a place of boundaries. Clearly, our species has pushed many of these boundaries and beyond. Our ever-increasing demand for earth's limited resources has led us down a dangerous pathway of no return, tearing away the delicate strata of life on which we all depend. In an age of enlightenment, why are we still losing ground on which we stand?

Many blame corporate and government entities, but blame does not fall on the heads of a few.

In the last century, we left our agrarian lifestyle behind, trading our kinship to the land for a lifeless relationship with technology. It is a perplexing time for us all, living in a world of machines, but still entirely dependent on the environment. Spending much of our time trapped behind walls of concrete and steel, we have become desensitized to a planet in peril. While we may be better aware of the plight, our species turns a blind eye and continues on a reckless course of consumerism, exhausting the planet's finite resources. The transfer of this uncertainty to our children has implications that are far worse. According to Richard Louv, author of "Last Child in the Woods," an exceptional book about our human disconnect to the natural world, the lack of connectivity to planet Earth has created a generation that may well be suffering a non-medical condition aptly labeled "nature-deficit disorder".

Environmental ethics is not a way to imagine. It is a way of life; a life that honors earth and its inhabitants; a life that considers no less than the whole. The decisions we make every day, singly or collectively, have far-reaching and sometimes irreversible consequences to the land; land that our progeny and fellow creatures will inherit. If we are to protect the things around us, we must all think in terms of how our every action, from flushing our toilets to the foods we eat, affects our planet and the life force within it.

Becoming better stewards of the land, air and water makes sense, regardless of climate change.

Caring for the environment is everybody's responsibility. If we fail as competent caretakers of our native soil, all that follows, including our children, will surely suffer the consequences.

Sustainable Development
The term "sustainable development" promotes the ridiculous idea that Earth's finite resources can continue to be developed indefinitely. Continued development of limited resources is not sustainable! An excerpt from the document, *Global Diversity Strategies* has this to say; "Development has to be both people-centered and conservation based. Unless we protect the structure, function, and diversity of the world's natural systems—on which our species and all others depend—development will undermine itself and fail. Unless we use our Earth's resources sustainably and prudently, we deny people their future. Development must not come at the expense of other groups or later generations, nor threaten other species' survival (WRI 1992)". In many regions of the world, human population now exceeds the land's capacity to sustain life without the support of international intervention.

Humanity now stands at the crossroads of choice; one that leads to an unpleasant and devastating journey or one that remains truly balanced and sustainable for generations to come.

The world as seen through the eyes of a child

PICTORIAL DESCRIPTION OF TERMS

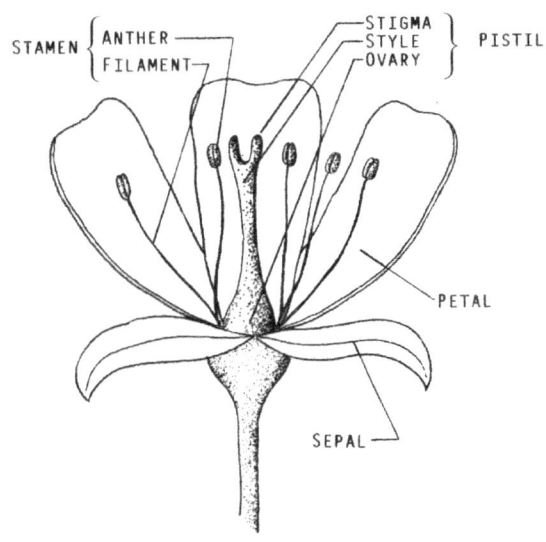

FLOWER STRUCTURE (above): The pistil, the female part of the flower, includes the stigma, style and ovary. After fertilization, the ovary expands and forms the fruit of the plant. The male organs of the flower are the stamens and are made up of two parts: filament and anther. In most flowers, the reproductive parts are surrounded by two sets of floral structures: petals (can be any color) and sepals (usually green).

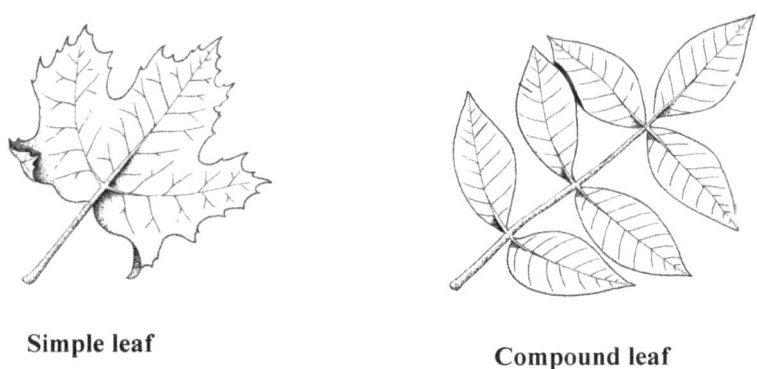

Simple leaf   Compound leaf

LEAF TYPES (above): The two basic leaf types used in this book are simple and compound. Simple leaves are single leaves, as in maple and oak leaves. Compound leaves are made up of many leaflets, as in walnut and ash leaves.

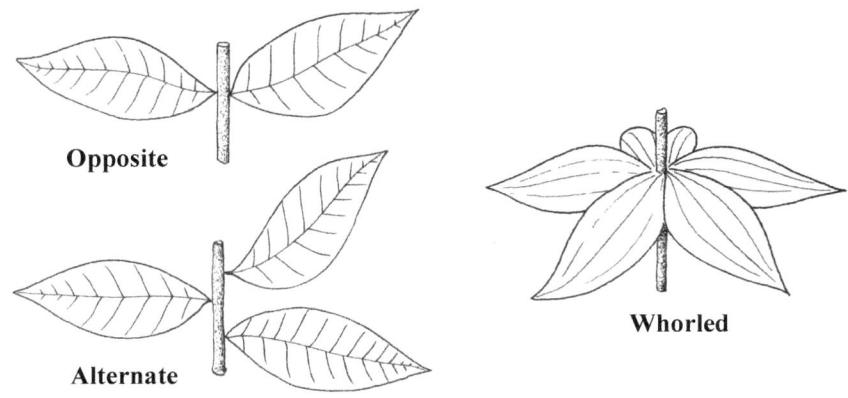

LEAF ARRANGEMENT (Above): the arrangement of the leaves are on the stem are opposite, alternate or whorled.

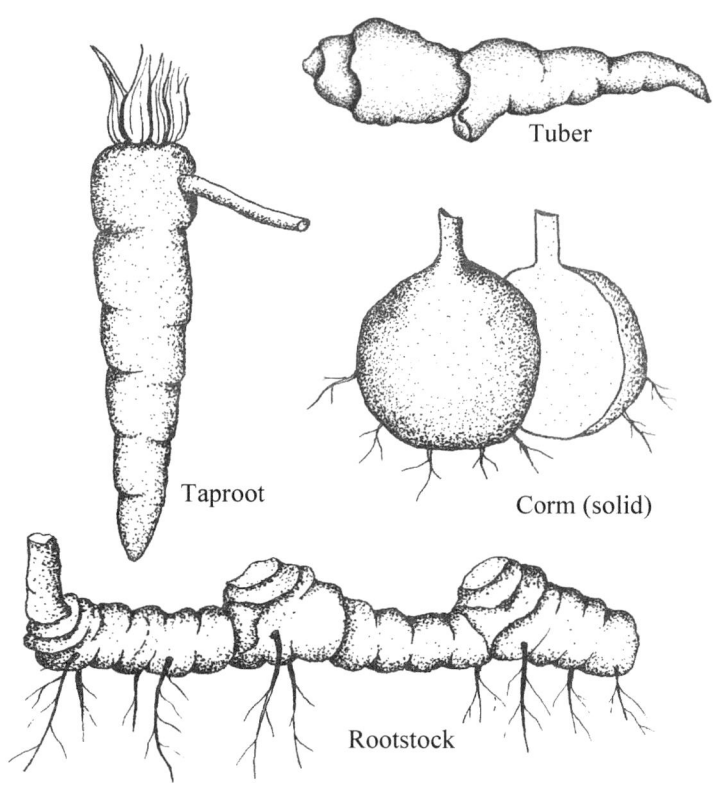

ROOTS (Figure D): Basic root types include: taproot, corm, rootstock and tuber. They vary greatly in size, shape and direction of growth.

WILD EDIBLE PLANTS of EASTERN KENTUCKY

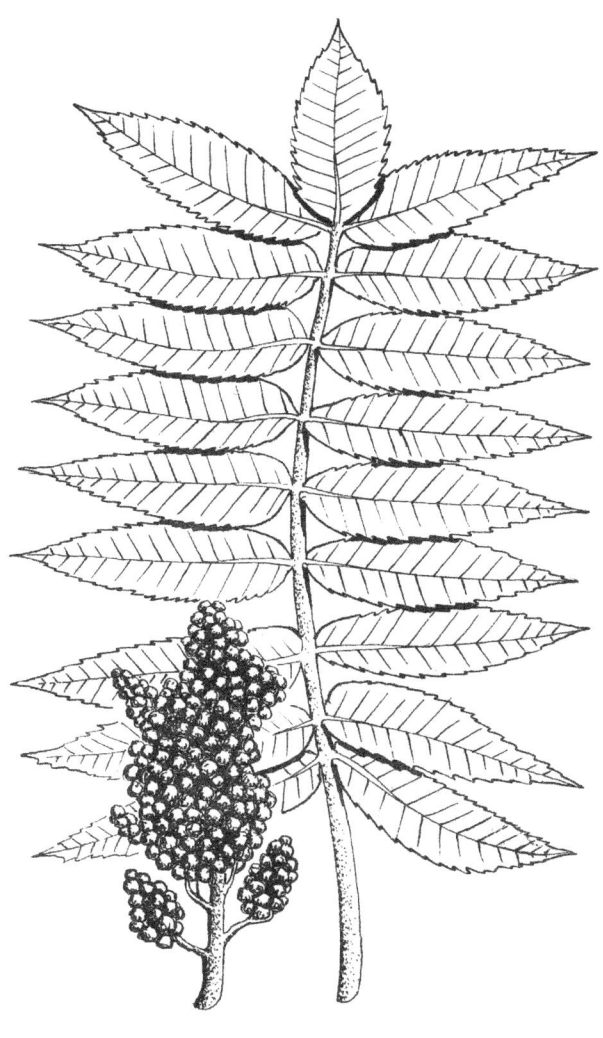

COMMON GREENBRIER
(Smilax rotundifolia)

IDENTIFICATION AND HABITAT
The Common Greenbrier is a vine found clinging to small trees and shrubs. It grows best on dry ridgetops where it will often create tangles in clearings and open woodlands. Leaves are broadly-rounded or heart-shaped, simple, alternate and 1-3/4 to 4 inches long. Stems are round or angled and armed with very convincing prickles.

EDIBLE PARTS
<u>Tendrils</u>: young tendrils have a tart-sour taste that makes a delicious snack when hiking. <u>Shoots and leaves</u>: young shoots and leaves can be steamed like any garden vegetable or eaten raw. So next time you're backpacking in Eastern Kentucky and a Greenbrier snags your leg, just reach over and take a bite out of it!!

BEST TIME TO HARVEST: Spring (tendrils, shoots and leaves). Summer (tendrils and shoots).

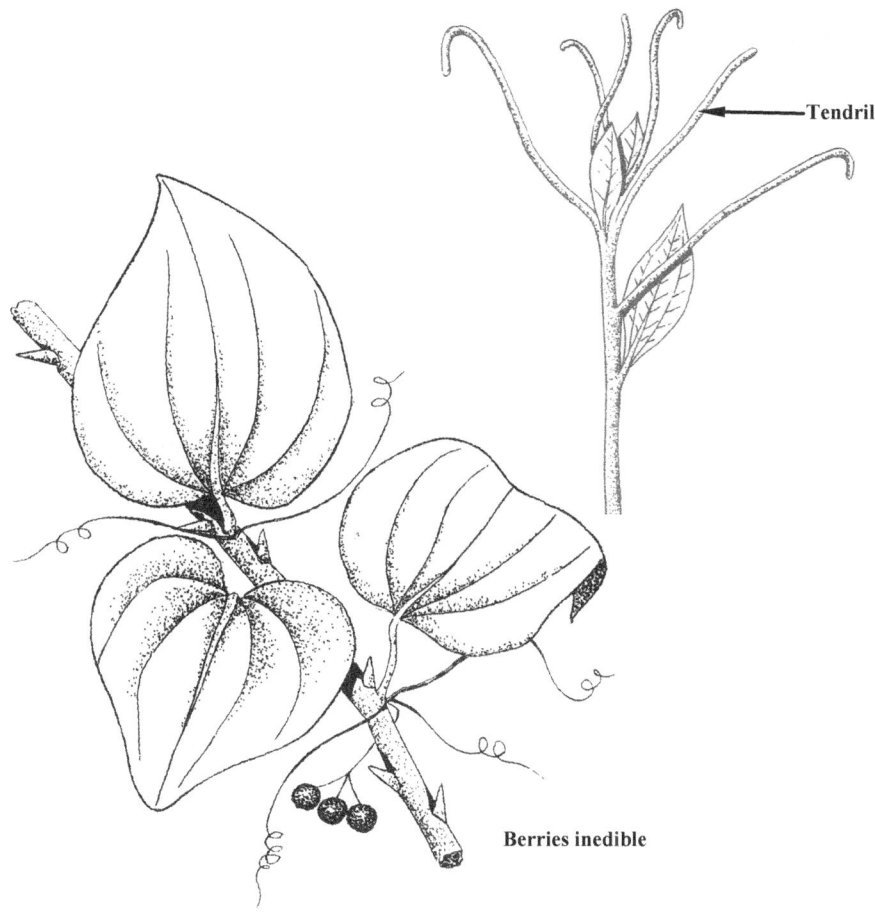
Tendril
Berries inedible

REDBUD
(Cercis canadensis)

IDENTIFICATION AND HABITAT
The Redbud is considered a shrub or small tree. It is one of the first trees to flower in the spring shortly after the Serviceberry and a few weeks earlier than Dogwoods. The Redbud can be found growing on roadsides (especially along the Mountain Parkway), forest edges, and to a lesser degree, inside wooded areas. Leaves are large, alternate and heart-shaped. Flowers have four or five petals, hang in large clusters and are red-purple or occasionally white. Redbuds are an excellent native shrub for any yard.

EDIBLE PARTS
Flowers: The brightly colored fresh flowers found can be eaten raw or added to a bowl of salad for a splash of color and nutrition. Leaves: Young leaves can be eaten raw or cooked. Seed Pods: Young pods can be steamed or sautéed. The flowers and the seeds are very high in antioxidants as well as linoleic and alpha-linolenic acid (Hunter et al. 2006). So, this spring when the redbuds are blooming, grab a handful of redbud flowers for your enjoyment and health!

BEST TIME TO HARVEST: Spring (flowers and leaves). Summer (Pods).

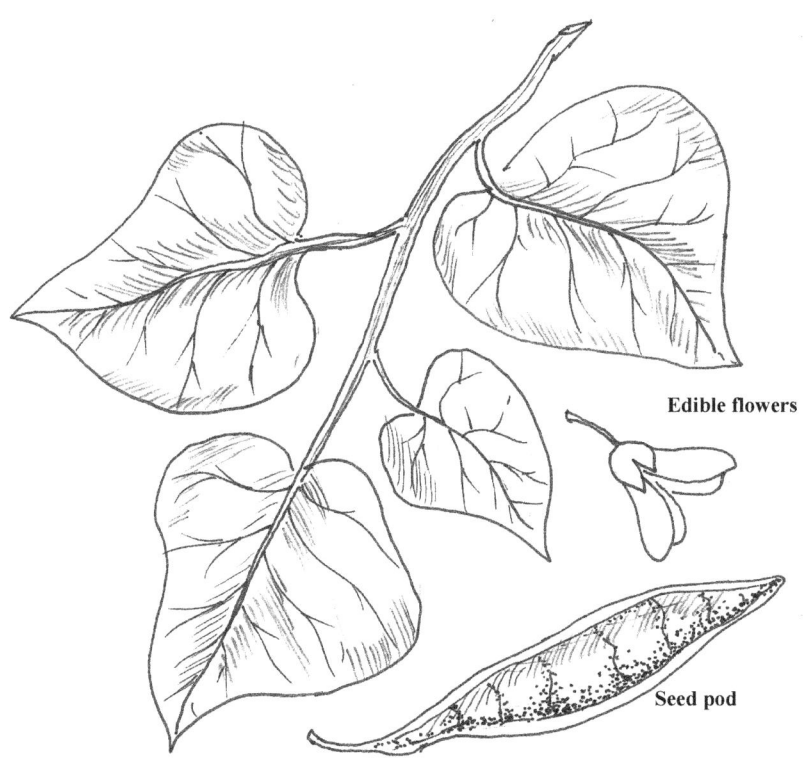

TOOTHWORT
(Cardamine species)

IDENTIFICATION AND HABITAT
Several species of Toothwort occur in the Eastern Kentucky area. All are low growing herbs of rich sites such as steep-sided ravines and hillsides. Leaves are in sets of three, pointed and serrated, 2-3 inches long. Flowers have four petals and are usually white.

EDIBLE PARTS
Flowers: Young flowers and leaves can be eaten raw or added to salads. Leaves: Leaves of some species are peppery-hot but this varies from site to site depending on soil chemistry. As with any edible, it is best to take a small taste at first. Roots: The somewhat crispy pungent tasting roots can also be eaten raw or cooked. Native Americans cleaned the roots, placed them on a blanket and covered them allowing the roots to ferment four or five days which creates a sweet more palatable taste. We put the flowers and leaves in our smoothies for the extra nutrient boost.

BEST TIME TO HARVEST: Spring (flowers and leaves). Anytime (roots).

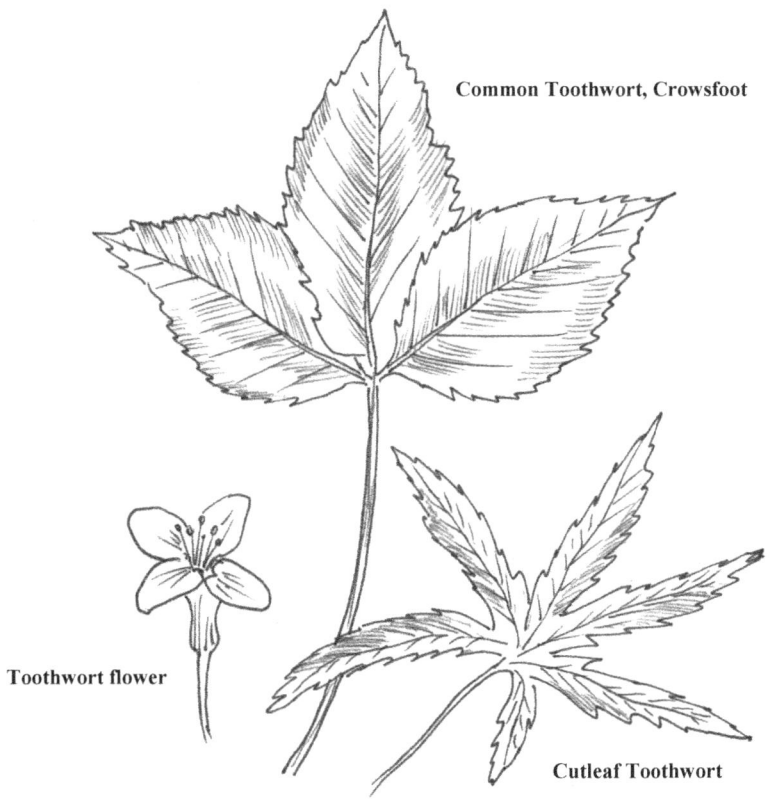
Common Toothwort, Crowsfoot
Toothwort flower
Cutleaf Toothwort

DANDELION
(Tararacum officinale)

IDENTIFICATION AND HABITAT
The much maligned Dandelion is actually a marvelous edible which can be used in everyday cooking. Although considered a weed by most its an herb with many medicinal proprieties. Habitat includes just about any open space. Leaves are deeply notched and. flowers have numerous yellow petals.

EDIBLE PARTS
Flowers: Blossoms can be batter-dipped and fried, tasting even better than fried mushrooms!
Leaves: Young leaves can be added to salads raw or cooked like spinach.
Roots: Roots can be roasted and ground to make a coffee-like drink. Scrub roots, drain and place on a baking sheet. Roast at 150 F until roots are dark and dry (about 4 hours). Cool. Store in covered jar. Grind dried roots and use as a coffee substitute. We actually planted this delightful herb in our yard, adding the vitamin-packed leaves to morning smoothies all summer long. Dandelions are rich in nutrients including protein, calcium, iron and Vitamins A & C.

BEST TIME TO HARVEST: Spring (flowers and leaves). Anytime (roots).

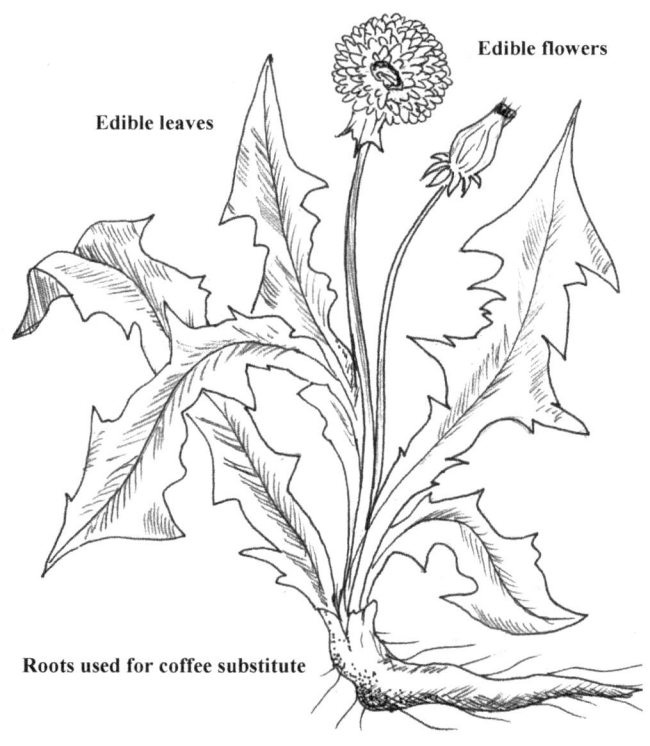

PARTRIDGEBERRY, BANKBERRY
(Mitchella repens)

IDENTIFICATION AND HABITAT
The Partridgeberry is a small, low-growing evergreen plant which is fairly common throughout Eastern Kentucky. The species can be found growing on shaded cliffsides as well as banks near trails and old access roads. Leaves are paired, roundish, 1/3 to 2/3 inches long and may be variegated with whitish lines. Flowers have four petals and are either pink or white.

EDIBLE PARTS
Fruit: Red berries can be eaten as found or added to salads. Although the berries are dry, seedy and bland, they are quite nutritious and offer a source of winter food. Leaves: Leaves and berries can be dried and made into a tea. American Indian women consumed this tea during childbirth. Strain through cheesecloth to remove any undesired material. The Partridgeberry can be planted as an edible ornamental in your yard in shaded areas.

BEST TIME TO HARVEST: Summer-Early Winter (fruits and leaves).

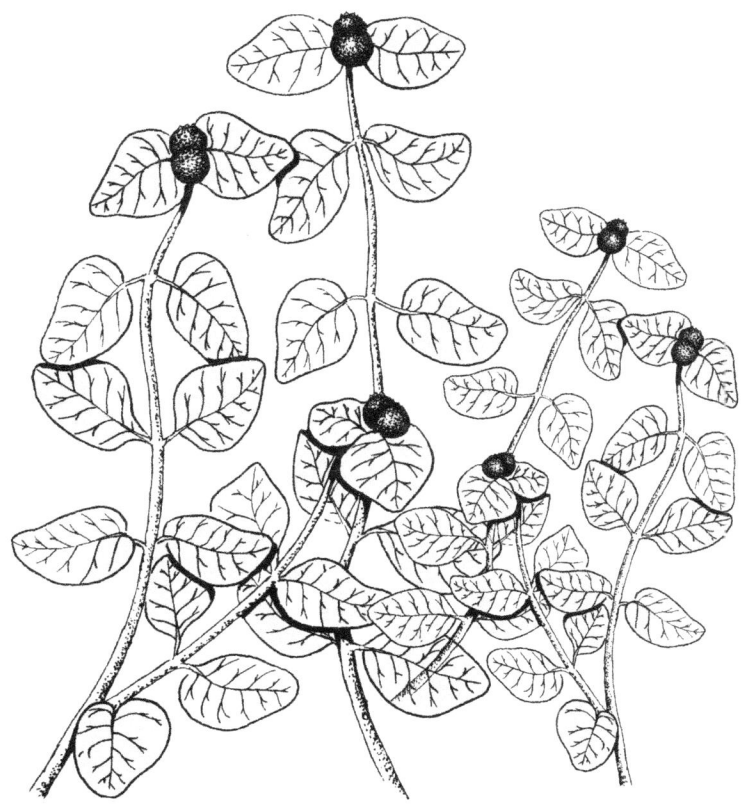

SERVICEBERRY, SARVIS
(Amelanchier arborea)

IDENTIFICATION AND HABITAT
The Serviceberry is a shrub to low-growing tree and is fairly prevalent in the area. About mid-April, the white flowers of the tree can easily be observed on cliff edges throughout the gorge. Dry sandstone ridgetops provide the species its best habitat. Leaves are simple, alternate, oval in shape, 1 3/4 to 3 1/2 inches long and moderately toothed. As legend would have it, the name Serviceberry may have come from a past era when graves were dug by hand, not backhoes. People who died during winter months were placed in an outbuilding because the ground was too hard to dig. Come springtime folks knew it was time to bury the dead when the serviceberry was in flower, a sign that the frozen ground had thawed enough to dig a grave, at which time "services" for the dead were conducted.

EDIBLE PARTS
Fruit: In June, serviceberry produces purple-black berries resemble the taste of blueberries with a hint of almond and are as sweet as sorghum. Just eat as is or add to pancakes. Serviceberry was also added to minced dried meat and fat to make the Native American travel food, pemmican. Trees found near and around clearings in the gorge will tend to be more productive because increased sunlight stimulates flower growth and thus increases berry production. In fact, this is true with most species of plants being exposed to more sunlight.

BEST TIME TO HARVEST: June (fruit).

BLACKBERRIES
(*Rubus* species)

IDENTIFICATION AND HABITAT
Blackberries are a common resident needing little description. Found growing along wooded edges, wildlife opening and fence rows, blackberries are an important food source for a wide range of wildlife species. Leaves are in sets of three, serrated and pointed, 2-3 inches long. Flowers are typically white. Other species in this large family that occur locally include the native Black Raspberry and the often-planted Red Raspberry (also known as Wineberry). Like the Blackberry, both species have delightfully sweet berries.

EDIBLE PARTS
<u>Shoots:</u> The young edible shoots are harvested in the spring, peeled and used in salads. <u>Fruit:</u> Blackberry fruits are not ripe enough to eat until they are a deep purple-black. There's an old expression, "blackberries are red when they're green!" The ripest, sweetest berries are easily pulled from the vine while the tart ones are more difficult to pull. Blackberries are an excellent source of dietary fiber, vitamins C and K. Blackberry seeds are large and not always preferred by the consumer but they are rich in Omega-3 and 6 fats as well as proteins. In addition, research has shown that consumption of deep-colored fruits and vegetables that contain a powerhouse of phytochemicals (anti-oxidants) also produce health benefits to the consumer. These berries pack a nutritional punch that should not be ignored!

BEST TIME TO HARVEST: Spring (shoots). Mid-July to early August (fruits).

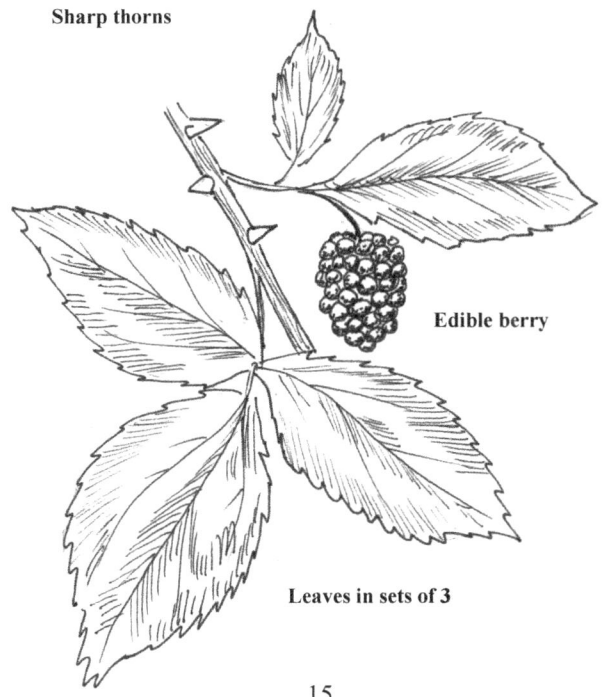

BLUEBERRIES & HUCKLEBERRIES
(Vaccinium species)

IDENTIFICATION AND HABITAT
The wild Blueberry and Huckleberry of eastern North America belong to a large family, *Vaccinum* with at least 6 species in the Gorge and the Greater Red River Basin. The Blueberry is a bush that grows up to 6 feet while the huckleberry is a low growing shrub of up to 2 feet. Both species grow on sandstone ridgetops and cliff edges. Leaves can be either deciduous or evergreen. Flowers are bell-shaped, white, pale-pink or red, sometimes tinged greenish. Fruits differ in color with the ripe huckleberry taking on more of a reddish purple hue than the deep purple of the blueberry. The fruit is a berry covered in a protective coating of powdery epicuticular wax, colloquially known as the "bloom". The most productive plants in terms of berry-load occur where there has been a recent fire.

EDIBLE PARTS
<u>Fruit:</u> The fruit can be eaten raw or used in recipes. They have a sweet taste when mature, with variable acidity. A fond family tradition of ours included these delectable berries loaded with anti-oxidants and nutrition. Our disgruntled teenaged children were rousted out of bed for an early morning weekend hike up the cliffline to pick wild blueberries/huckleberries which we added to our whole wheat pancakes. While they never enjoyed the zombie-walks up the steep hill, they were always quite eager to gobble up the tasty pancakes! These berries are so pleasing to the taste buds that overeating is easy.

BEST TIME TO HARVEST: May-August (fruit). Blueberry/huckleberry bushes typically bear fruit in the middle of the growing season: fruiting times are affected by local conditions such as altitude and latitude, so the peak of the crop can vary from May to August (in the northern hemisphere) depending upon these conditions

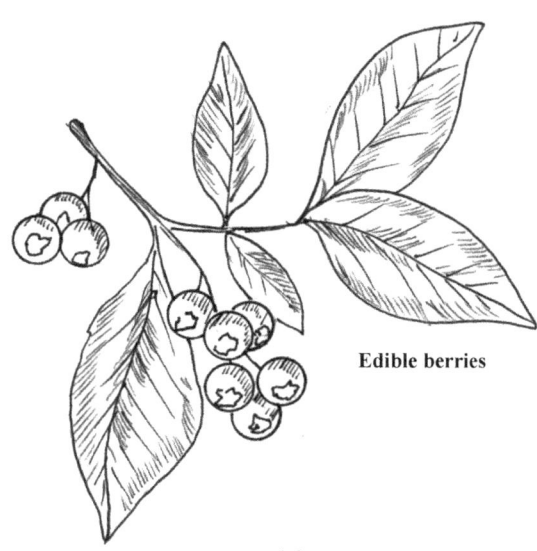
Edible berries

WILD STRAWBERRY, VIRGINIA STRAWBERRY
(Fragaria virginiana)

IDENTIFICATION AND HABITAT
Wild strawberry is a ground-hugging plant rising from a fibrous perennial root system. One of several wild varieties hybridized to produce the domestic variety, the wild strawberry fruit is somewhat smaller. Overall height of the plant is 2-6 inches. Leaves are long-stalked with three coarsely-toothed leaflets. A hairy flower stalk gives rise to a loose cluster of small five-petaled flowers that bloom in April. Found in patches of fields and dry openings this plant is commonly mistaken for the Indian Mock strawberry whose flowers are yellow instead of white and fruits have little or no taste. Contrary to popular belief, wild strawberries are not poisonous.

EDIBLE PARTS
Fruit: Wild strawberries are an excellent source of antioxidants, vitamins A, C, E and the B-complex group as well as minerals such as, potassium, manganese, fluorine, copper, iron and iodine Although Wild Strawberries tend to be considerably smaller than commercially grown varieties, what they lack in size is made up in taste. Wild Strawberries are much sweeter and offer the consumer a delightful change from their sometimes bitter and larger cousins. Leaves: A tea made from dried leaves is both pleasing and high in vitamin C. When making a tea, use cheesecloth or a tea ball to strain the leaves. Wild strawberries are a culinary delicacy and should be treated as such. They are also quite perishable and thus, will need to be utilized within a few days of harvest. They are as versatile in savory recipes as sweet.

BEST TIME TO HARVEST: Late spring to mid summer (fruits and leaves).

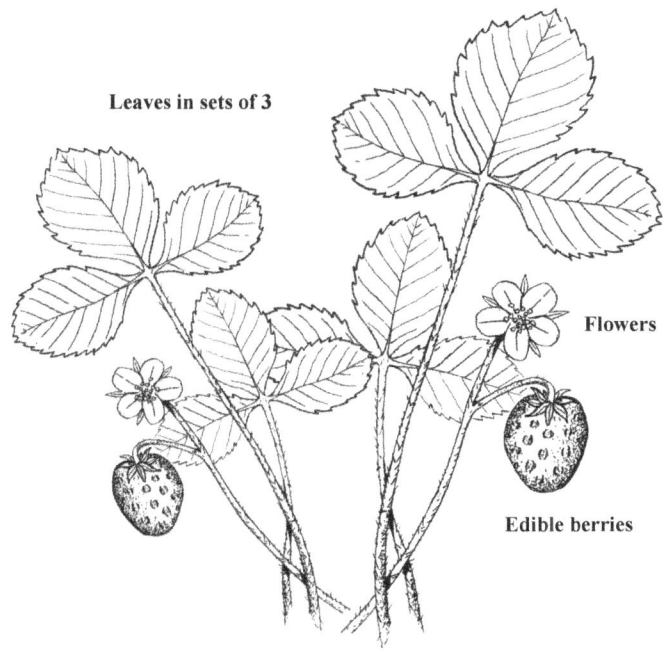

TEABERRY, AMERICAN WINTERGREEN
(Gaultheria procumbens)

IDENTIFICATION AND HABITAT
Teaberry or American Wintergreen is a low-growing evergreen plant that grows about 3-6 inches high. The thick shiny leaves, 1-2 inches long, are oval in shape and slightly toothed, having the odor of wintergreen when bruised. Flowers are small, white and egg-shaped. A calcifuge, it favors the acidic soils of pine or hardwood forests on dry ridgetops and clearings. Teaberry is quite common throughout the area but don't confuse it with partridgeberry (it's berries are bland) or other low-growing leafy plants that you may encounter. Remember the distinct taste and smell of wintergreen.

EDIBLE PARTS
Fruits: The ripe red berries and leaves of teaberry offer the unique taste and smell of mildly sweet wintergreen. Leaves: An excellent tea can be prepared from the fresh leaves. The leaves and branches make a fine herbal tea, through normal drying and infusion process. When making a tea, use cheesecloth or a tea ball to strain the leaves. The tender new spring leaves (light green in color) can be used as a trailside nibble. For the leaves to yield significant amounts of their essential oil, they need to be fermented for at least three days. Teaberry is also a flavor of ice cream and inspired the name of Clark's Teaberry chewing gum. The evergreen leaves provide a rare source of nutrition for animals in the winter.

BEST TIME TO HARVEST: Late summer all through the winter (fruits and leaves).

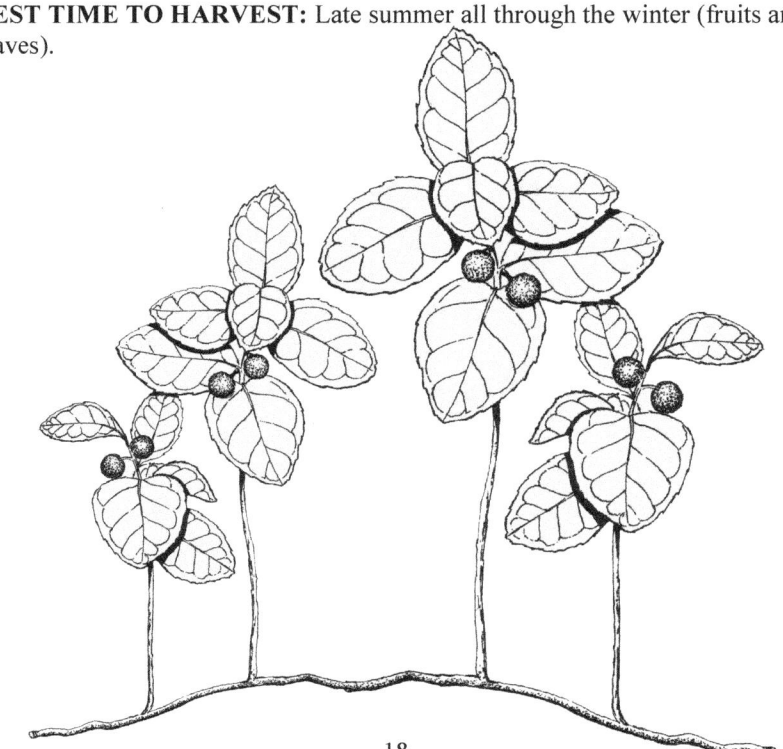

SUMAC
(*Asimina* species)

IDENTIFICATION AND HABITAT
The Sumacs are wonderful shrubs or small trees with large compound, alternate leaves, up to 24 inches long. Twigs are stout and pithy containing a milky sap. Clearings and old fields along wooded borders are good sites to hunt for sumacs. While Poison Sumac (*Rhus vernix*), a species of swamps, is quite poisonous on contact, it is not known to occur in eastern Kentucky. Four species occur in and around Eastern Kentucky including: Winged Sumac (*Rhus copallina*), Smooth Sumac (*Rhus glabra*), Staghorn Sumac (*Rhus typhina*) and Fragrant Sumac (*Rhus aromatic*). Berries of these four species are red whereas the berries of Poison Sumac are white. Sumac berries are an important source of winter food for ruffed grouse and wild turkey.

EDIBLE PARTS
Fruit: Berry clusters of mature Sumacs will form at the ends of the branches in fall. To make a beverage that tastes somewhat like lemonade, first collect the entire fruit cluster. Gather the fruit clusters before heavy rains wash out most of the acid content of the berries, this is the very thing that gives the drink its interesting flavor. Bruise the berries by rubbing gently between your hands. Then soak one berry cluster in an 8 ounce glass of cold water for 10-15 minutes. Remove the cluster of fruit and strain the juice through cheese cloth to remove loose berries and other bits. Or place 3-4 clusters in cheesecloth in glass gallon jug. Place in the sun for 8 hours to make a "tea" If desired, sweeten with honey and chill. Keep the mixture refrigerated.

BEST TIME TO HARVEST: Fall (fruits).

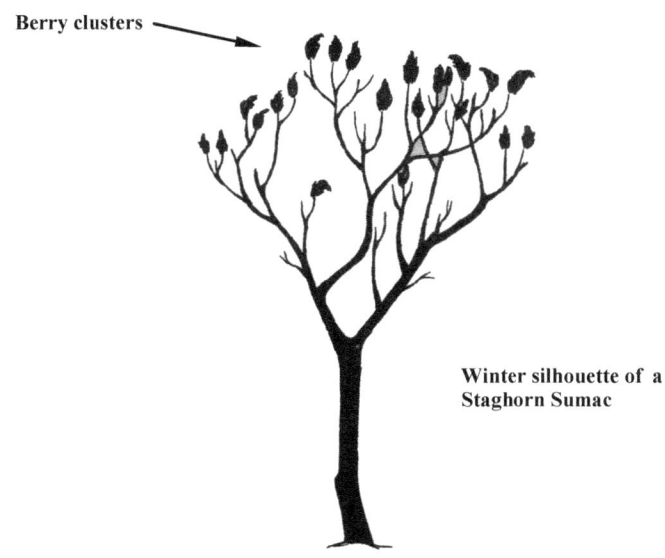

Berry clusters

Winter silhouette of a Staghorn Sumac

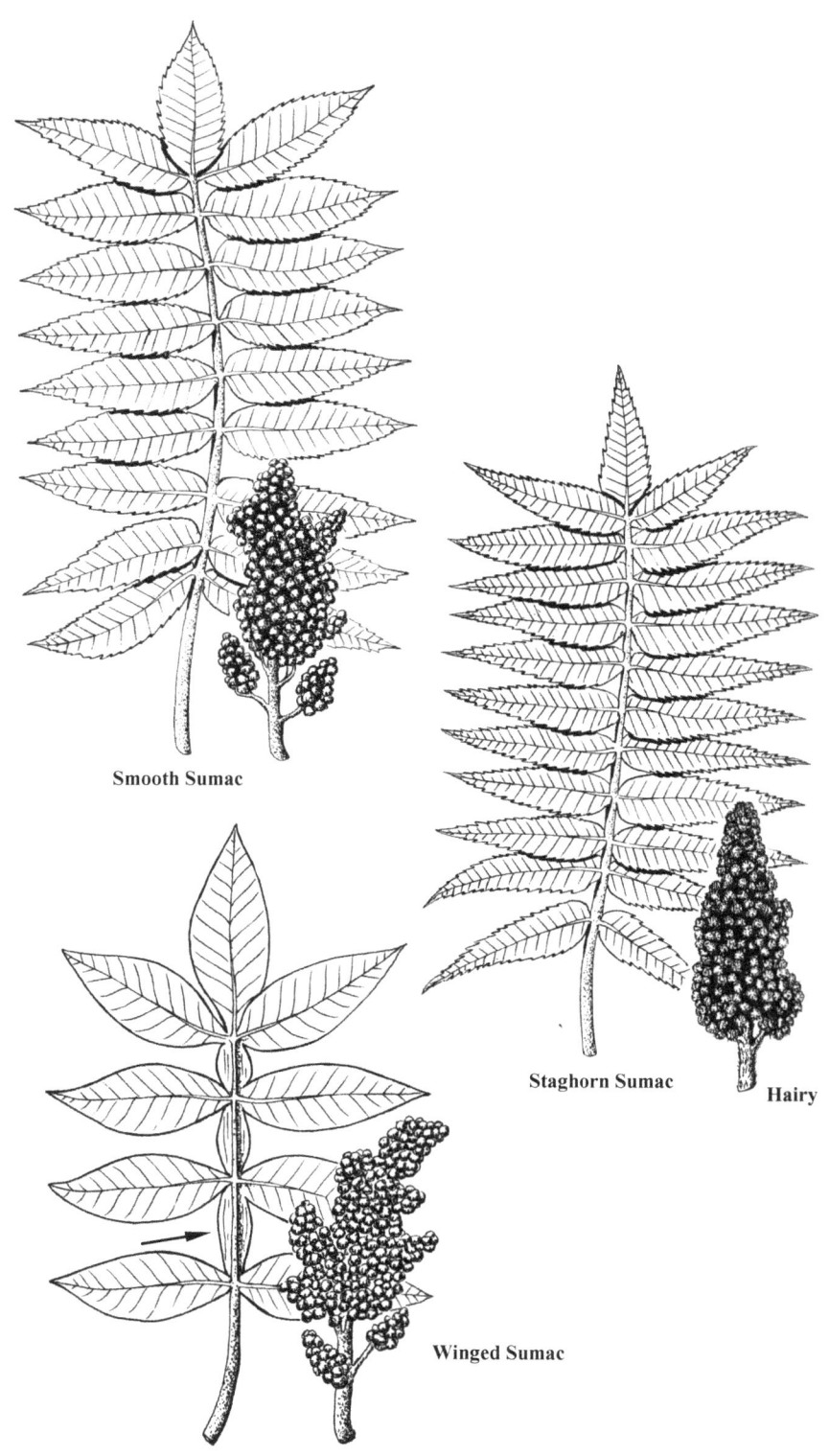

PERSIMMON, POSSUM BERRIES
(Diospyros virginiana)

IDENTIFICATION AND HABITAT
Although Persimmons grow in a variety of habitats, they tend to be mcst frequent in dry deciduous woods and old fields. The leaves are simple, alternate, 4-6 inches long, dark green above and pale green on their underside. Persimmons rarely grow over 50 feet tall, although if forest conditions are favorable, the species has reached heights in excess of 95 feet. Bark of the tree is quite dark and deeply divided into squarish blocks. The wood is like concrete and in the past was used to make golf-club heads.

EDIBLE PARTS
Fruit: If you have ever tasted an unripe persimmon, you would surely remember its unpleasant qualities. The contrast between a green and a truly ripe persimmon is hard to believe. When ripe, the fruit is extremely sweet and soft, having its own unusual flavor. Unripe, it will turn your mouth every which way but loose. Sometimes in late fall, the soft and pulpy, ripe persimmon can be eaten after removing the seeds. Disregard any hard fruit as it still retains a very unpleasant taste. Leaves: A fine rich tea high in vitamin C can be prepared from the dried leaves as well.

BEST TIME TO HARVEST: Spring to late fall (leaves). Late fall (fruits).

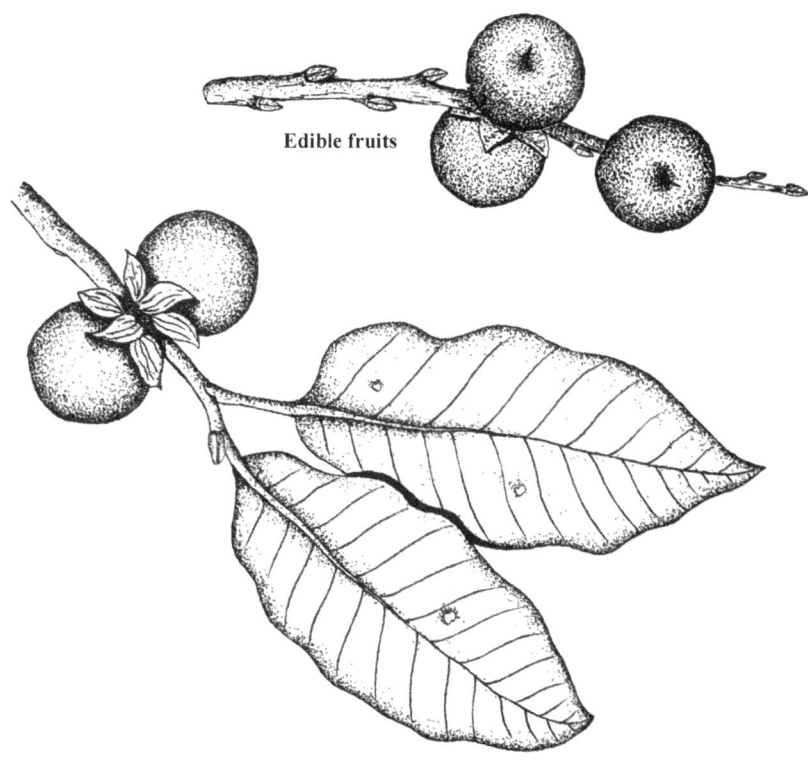
Edible fruits

PAWPAW, CUSTARD APPLE, POOR MAN'S BANANA
(*Asimina triloba*)

IDENTIFICATION AND HABITAT
The Pawpaw is a small, deciduous tree belonging to a family of plants that are predominantly tropical. Often forming thickets, Pawpaws are found in well-drained, deep, fertile bottom-land and hilly upland habitat. Leaves are simple, alternate, 6-12 inches long and foul-smelling when bruised. Flowers are 1-2 inches across, rich maroon when mature. Pawpaw fruits are the largest edible fruit indigenous to the United States.

EDIBLE PARTS
<u>Fruit:</u> When ripe, the large fruit of the pawpaw (2-6 inches long) is a deep yellow to brown berry and has a sweet custard flavor similar to banana, mango, and cantaloupe. It is commonly eaten raw and make a delicious ice cream. The yet-green pawpaws found on the tree can be set aside for a few days to ripen. When mature, the heavy yellow-brown fruits bend the weak branches of the tree. <u>Leaves:</u> Leaves can be ground into a natural pesticide for gardens and fruit trees. Pawpaw extract harvested from the twigs in May of year has proven to be effective as an anti-lice shampoo and against cancer cells in test tube studies, but inconclusive in human clinical studies (Memorial Sloan Kettering Cancer Center 2014).

BEST TIME TO HARVEST: May (twigs). September-October (fruits).

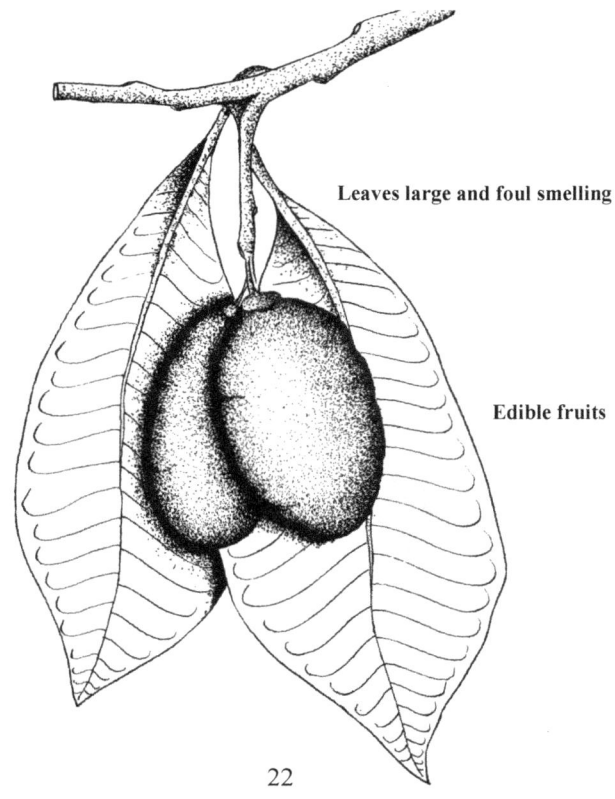

AMERICAN BEECH, INITIAL TREE
(Fagus grandifolia)

IDENTIFICATION AND HABITAT
A majestic tree among the eastern deciduous forests, the American Beech has widely spreading branches, a hollow trunk and prefers a habitat of rich moist soils in coves and steep-sided ravines. Early settlers often searched for beeches as a sign of a good potential place to clear the forest for farming. The smooth, light-gray bark and beech buds that are distinctly long and thin, resembling cigars are two characters that make identification easy. Leaves are simple, alternate, coarsely toothed and 1-5 inches long. The name "initial tree" comes from the practice of carving initials into the tree's smooth bark, which can last for decades. It can take up to 40 years for the tree to begin producing seeds.

EDIBLE PARTS
<u>Nuts:</u> The sweet-tasting nuts of the American Beech are both nutritious and easy to harvest. During the first frosty nights of October, the tree will drop its seeds to the ground. The nuts can then be gathered, husked, shelled and eaten as is or left in the shells and roasted over a campfire. The nuts can also be dried and stored for future consumption.

BEST TIME TO HARVEST: October-November (nuts).

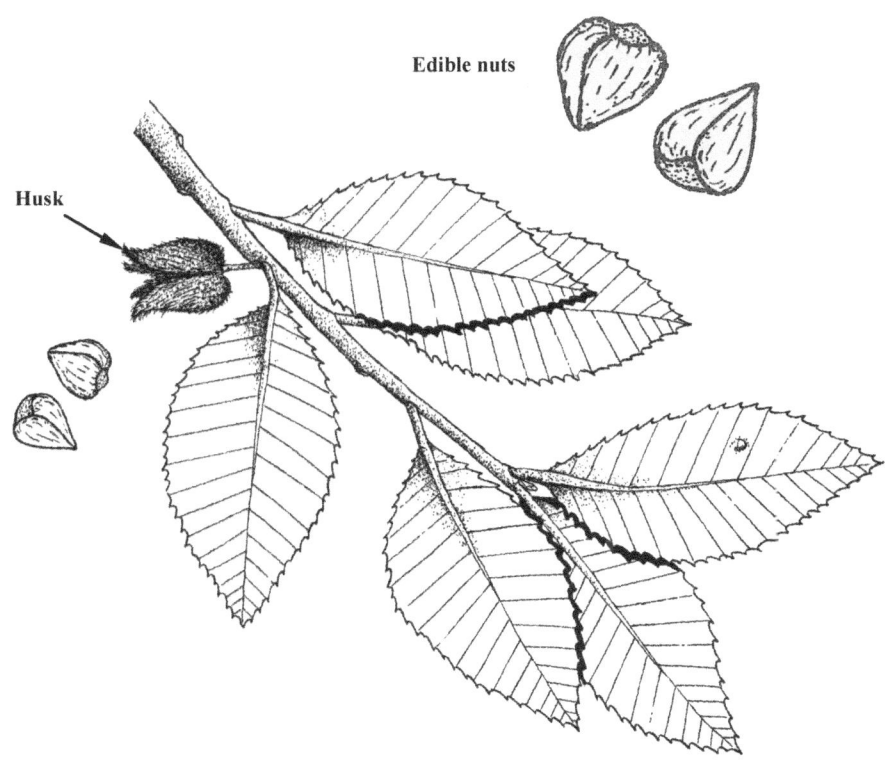

AMERICAN CHESTNUT
(Castenea dentata)

IDENTIFICATION AND HABITAT
Less than 75 years ago, the American Chestnut was one of the most magnificent and widespread trees of the eastern deciduous forests. Today it is nothing more than a few short-lived sprouts. The chestnut blight caused by an Asian bark fungus (*Cryphonectria parasitica*, formerly *Endothia parasitica*) all but wiped out the tree. Although sprouts from remnant stumps still persist, sometimes attaining heights of 30 feet or more, sadly the trees eventually fall victim to the ever-present blight. In this time span of 8-15 years, some young chestnuts occasionally produce edible nuts. Dry acid soils on upper slopes and ridgetops provide the chestnut tree the best habitat. The leaves are simple, alternate and sharply-toothed, 4-8 inches long, resembling that of Chestnut Oak leaves.

EDIBLE PARTS
Nuts: The sweet-tasting nuts can either be eaten raw (which I prefer) or roasted over a campfire. Husking the spiny nuts which contain anywhere from 1-3 nuts can be a real challenge. The best method I have used involves placing the spiny husks between your feet and using your shoes as a prying device. Husks will easily split open, exposing the inner nuts to be picked out. If you stumble upon an American chestnut that has borne some fruits while hiking, consider yourself lucky and enjoy this delicious, once-plentiful treat! Note: the American Chestnut Foundation has been working with researchers to develop a disease-resistant tree with the hopes of restoring this magnificent tree to the ecosystem where it was the most abundant tree in the forest.

BEST TIME TO HARVEST: September-October (nuts).

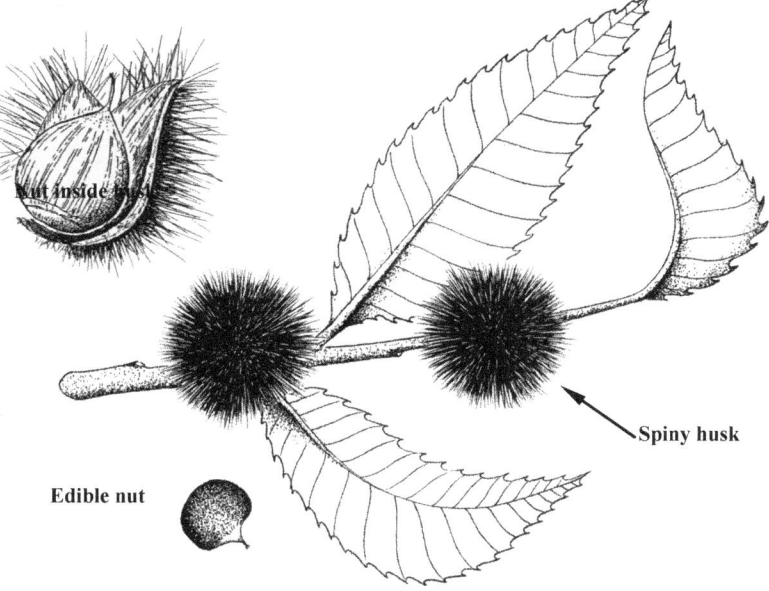

SHAGBARK HICKORY
(Carya ovata)

IDENTIFICATION AND HABITAT
The Shagbark Hickory is a large tree which grows best in river bottoms and upland slopes. Leaves are compound, alternate, averaging 5-7 leaflets (usually 5) and anywhere from 8-14 inches long. The red-brown twigs are stout and mostly hairless. One very important difference, as well as an aid for identification of the tree, is its very shaggy bark. It's easy to how this tree got its name! This characteristic will make it easy to identify this tree even from a distance.

EDIBLE PARTS
<u>Nuts:</u> The delicious nuts are a popular food among humans and squirrels alike. However, the length of time it takes for a tree to produce sizable crops (up to 40 years) and unpredictable output from year to year eliminates this nut from commercial production. After husking and shelling them, eat as is. The nuts are small and many chambered, making it slightly difficult to attain the meat, but your endeavors will be well-rewarded. Nuts can be used as a substitute for pecans and have nearly the same culinary function. Bark: Since Shagbark hickory bark naturally sloughs off, it can be easily harvested without harming the tree. American Indians boiled shagbark hickory bark to make sugar. The bark can be warmed/toasted in the oven. Amazingly, Shagbark hickory bark makes a delicious unique ice cream with a buttery, nutty, smoky flavor when boiled with milk and left to infuse. Recipe for this tasty treat can be found online at www.seriouseats.com.

BEST TIME TO HARVEST: October-November (nuts). Anytime (bark).

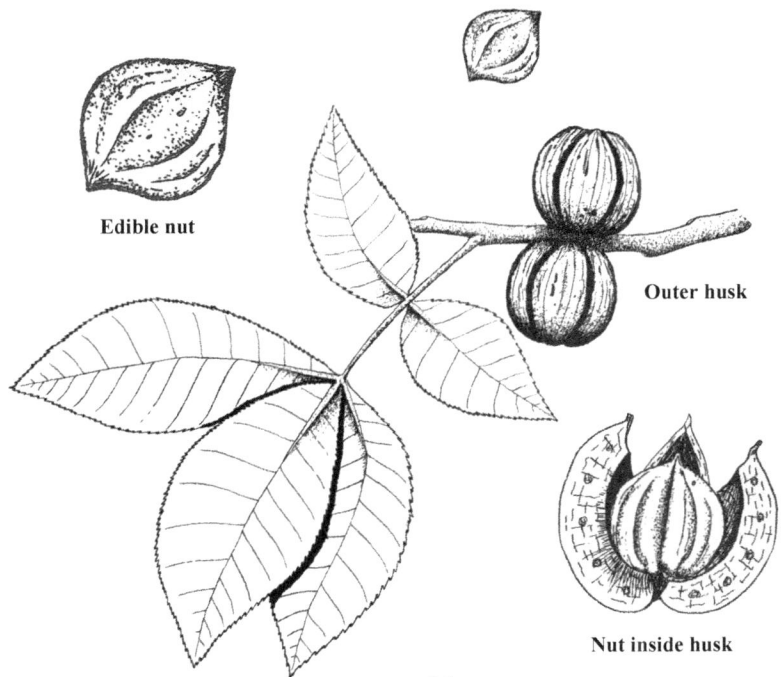

WHITE OAK
(Quercus alba)

IDENTIFICATION AND HABITAT
The Oaks comprise quite a large percentage of trees found in much of Eastern Kentucky. The White Oak is featured here because of its sweeter nuts and ease of identification. It is a sizeable tree up to 100 feet in height with grayish, scaly bark. Its leaves are simple, alternate, 4-8 inches long with the depth of lobing of the leaves varying greatly. The species prefers upper slopes and ridgetops and is common throughout the area.

EDIBLE PARTS
<u>Nuts</u>: You may have been told that acorns are poisonous but this is false. Actually, when prepared correctly, they are quite edible, very nutritious and rich in proteins and fats. Unprepared acorns are bitter and unpleasant tasting. This is because of the high concentration of tannin found within the nut. However, the tannin is readily soluble in water. Remove the husks, chop the meat inside into smaller pieces (this will allow the tannins to leach out more rapidly) then boil in several changes of water until water is clear. The nuts can then be roasted on a campfire and eaten as is, dipped in honey or ground into a flour.

BEST TIME TO HARVEST: October-November (nuts).

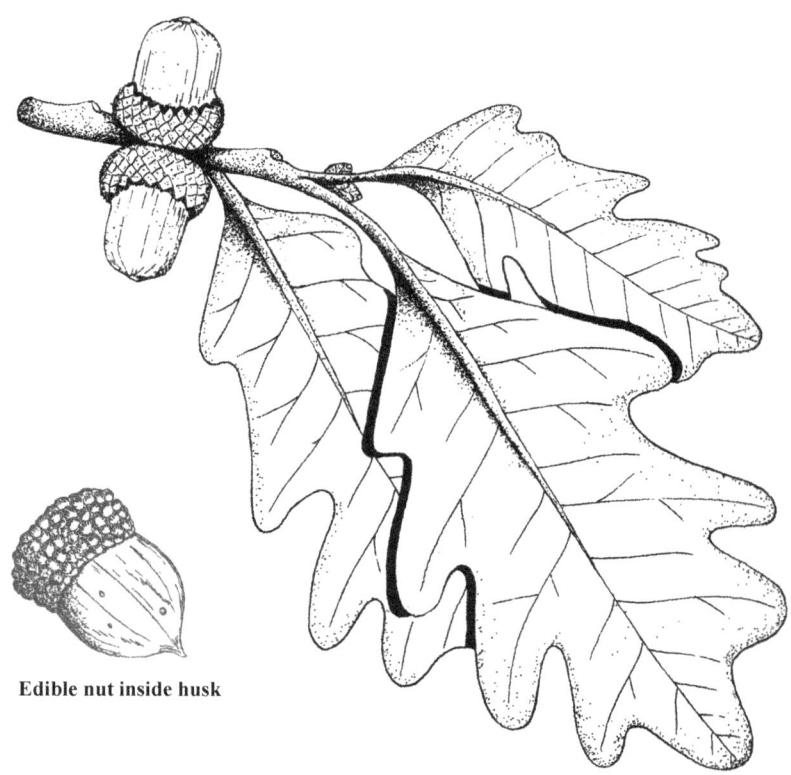

Edible nut inside husk

AMERICAN HAZELNUT
(Corylus americana)

IDENTIFICATION AND HABITAT
Characteristically forming dense thickets, the American Hazelnut is a shrub anywhere from 4-10 feet tall. It grows in a variety of habitats but most often is found near and around the streams and woodland borders. The leaves of the species are simple, alternate, 3-4 inches long and moderately toothed.

EDIBLE PARTS
You are indeed a fortunate person to happen upon a productive Hazelnut shrub. The easily harvested nuts of the species are of excellent taste and quality, closely resembling the European hazelnut or filbert. When ripe (sometime in October), the nuts can be eaten as is or dried for future use.

BEST TIME TO HARVEST: July-October (nuts).

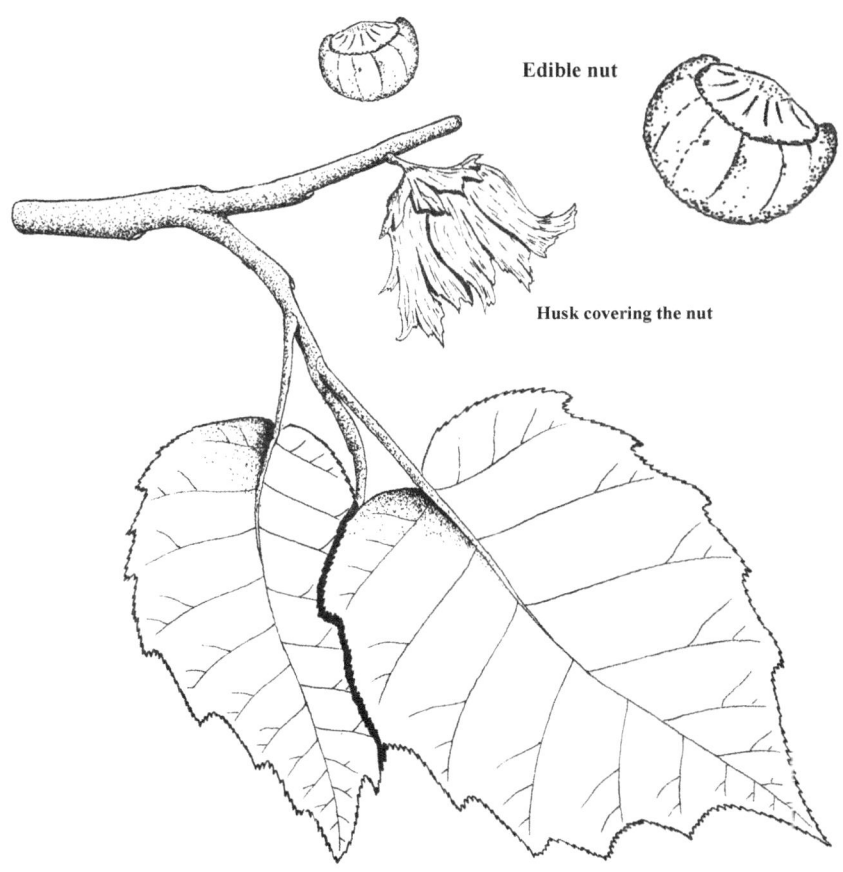

COMMON CATTAIL
(Typha latifolia)

IDENTIFICATION AND HABITAT
The Common Cattail might be one of the most nutritious wild edibles found in Eastern Kentucky. Often forming thickets, the tall plant grows up to 10 feet mostly in moist areas such as bogs, marshes and ponds. The long thin leaves of the Common Cattail tightly hug its base, feathering out towards the top. One of the more obvious characteristics of the species is its cigar-shaped flower spike.

EDIBLE PARTS
Different parts of the cattail can be utilized during all four seasons, offering the consumer a variety of interesting tastes. Shoots: The young shoots can be peeled to expose the tender white core and eaten raw or steamed like any young spring stalks while older shoots anywhere from 2-3 feet tall can also be prepared in much the same way. Shoots can also be pickled like cucumbers. Flowers: Late spring brings on the green immature flower spikes which should be gathered just before they erupt from their leafy sheaths. Boiled a minutes and served with butter, they taste somewhat like sweet corn. Roots: The starchy rootstocks of cattails grow close to the surface. Wash well and bake, roast or boil in a pot till soft. Upon eating the roots, you will accumulate some fibrous materials which can be discarded.

BEST TIME TO HARVEST: Early Spring (shoots and roots). Late Spring (flowers). Fall-Winter (Roots).

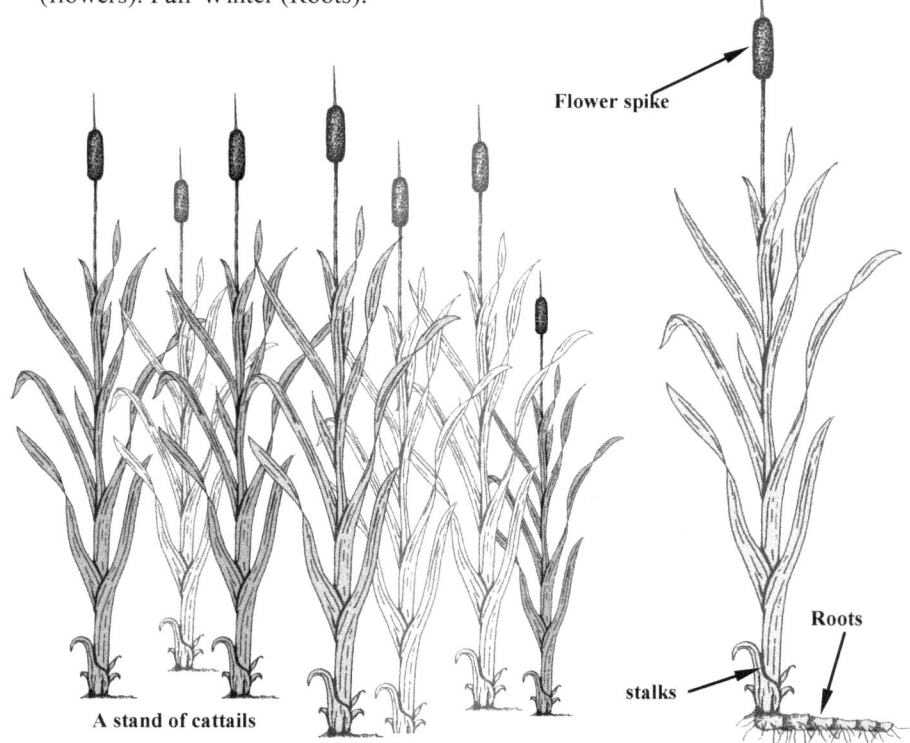

A stand of cattails

INDIAN CUCUMBER, CLEAR ROOT
(Medeola virginiana)

IDENTIFICATION AND HABITAT
An interesting forest plant, Indian Cucumber has a single stem with a whorl of 5-9 leaves, 2-5 inches long half-way up the stalk. If it is a mature plant, it will be topped by a second smaller whorl of usually three leaves, 1-2 inches long. Flowers are yellowish-green. The fruit is a dark blue to purple, inedible berry. Growing anywhere from 1-3 feet tall, the species thrives best in moist, shaded coves along streams and is common throughout the gorge. Indian Cucumber may be confused with the Whorled Pogonia (*Isotria verticillata*) which is an orchid growing the area as well. The stem of the Pogonia is succulent, hollow and without hairs whereas the Indian Cucumber has a wiry, slightly hairy stem. Deep purple berries are NOT edible.

EDIBLE PARTS
<u>Roots:</u> The tuber of Indian Cucumber or Clear Root is the only edible part of the plant and is usually found in the top 2-3 inches of soil, requiring a minimum of digging. It is crisp, watery and downright tasty! No preparation is necessary for consumption. Gather only when found in abundance; dig only the older plants leaving the younger ones to mature (see images below for comparison). This will better ensure the plant's existence for future consumers as well as observers.

BEST TIME TO HARVEST: Spring-Summer (roots).

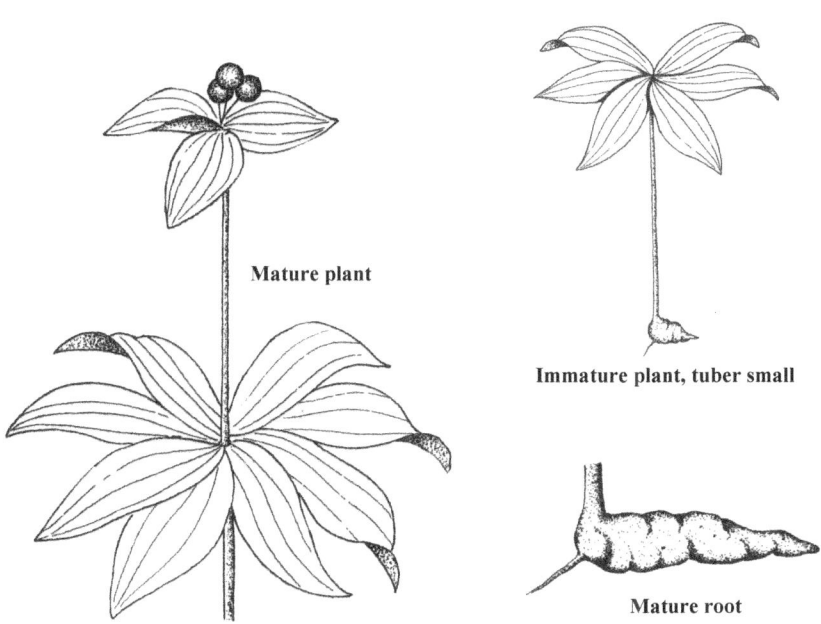

PINE TREES
(Pinus species)

IDENTIFICATION AND HABITAT
A widespread family of evergreen trees, the pines comprise one of the most vital groups of wild edibles in the world. All pines have edible parts and can be utilized in all four seasons. Some characteristics of the family are clusters of long slender needles bound at their base with anywhere from 2-5 needles per bundle. Woody cones ranging in many sizes and shapes are other similarities of the family. Most of the pines in Eastern Kentucky will be found on upper slopes and ridgetops where they prefer the dry acid conditions of the soil. There are four species common in the area: white pine *Pinus strobes* (illustrated below) pitch pine *Pinus rigida,* shortleaf pine *Pinus echinata,* and Virginia pine *Pinus virginiana*.

EDIBLE PARTS
Needles: The bright green new needles found near the tips of the branches can be used to make a tea that is high in Vitamins A and C. To prepare, simply chop the needles finely and steep in hot water for 10-15 minutes. Strain through cheesecloth to remove any undesired material. Add a sweetener if desired. Grapeseed or canola oil can be infused with dried pine needles to produce an aromatic base for salad dressing or brushing on grilled fish or chicken.
Cones: The woody cones contain small edible seeds which mature in fall. It is important to collect the cones before they open and release the nuts to the wild. After collecting the cones, roast over a fire or set aside for a few days until they pop open. Then simply pick or shake the nuts out and eat as is.

BEST TIME TO HARVEST: Spring (needles). Fall (cones).

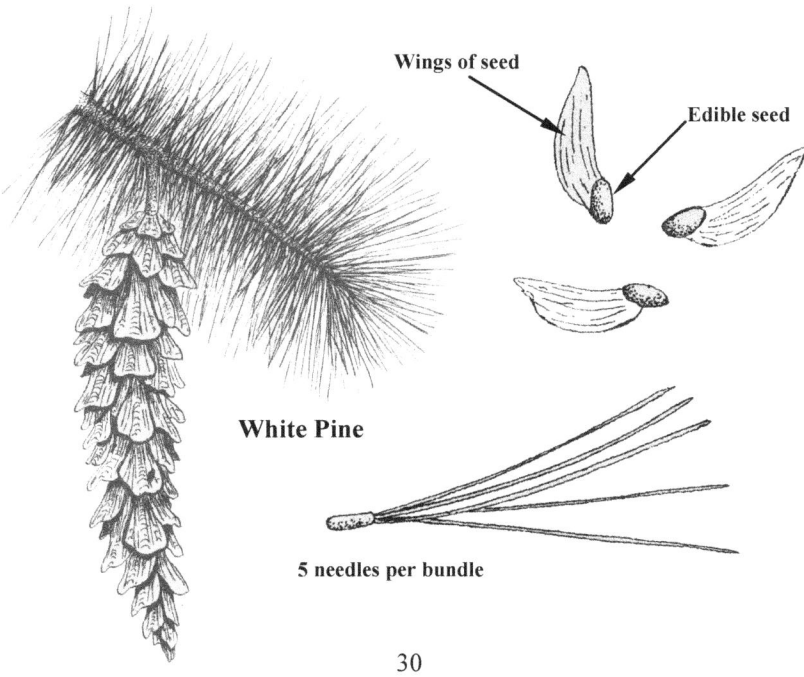

White Pine

5 needles per bundle

COMMON MOREL, DRY LAND FISH
(Morchella esculenta)

IDENTIFICATION AND HABITAT
Morel Mushrooms, in the genus Morchella, the true morels, is an edible sac fungi closely related to a simpler cup fungi. These distinctive fungi have a honeycomb appearance, due to the network of ridges with pits composing the cap. are probably the best known and most sought of all the edible fungi and with good reason. They have an excellent texture, superbly absorbing the flavors in which they are cooked. I have been told that the best places to find the fungi is under old dead Elm trees but I have had the best luck on rich hillside covered in large Tulip Poplar. In any case, the morels seem to grow in a variety of habitats. All true morels are edible (I know of 3 species in the area) and Be careful not to confuse True Morels with the sometimes encountered False Morels (which are typically inedible or even poisonous). The best way to distinguish between the two is the cap of True Morels is attached directly to the stalk (page 32).

EDIBLE PARTS
Fruiting body: Always consume cooked morels. NEVER eat them raw as they contain toxic substances that destroy red blood cells. These toxins are rendered harmless during cooking. Dry Land Fish or Common Morels can be prepared like domesticated mushrooms. To best enhance and enjoy the flavor, I recommend a simple preparation. Split the morels lengthwise in half. Rinse thoroughly in order to remove any debris or insects. Soak in salt water for at least an hour. Dip in egg then shake in a Ziploc bag with flour and seasonings of your choice. Use butter or coconut oil to fry the battered morels until golden brown. The texture and flavor is truly one of nature's finest.

BEST TIME TO HARVEST: Spring (fruiting body). Go hunting before the trees have fully leaved out, after a rain with a warm night to follow. Surprisingly, this combination of warm, wet weather seems to generate growth overnight. I have scoured a hillside looking for the morels without success, returning to the same site a day or two later to find more morels than I could carry. Always avoid morel-like mushrooms of Summer and Fall. All True Morels fruit in the spring!

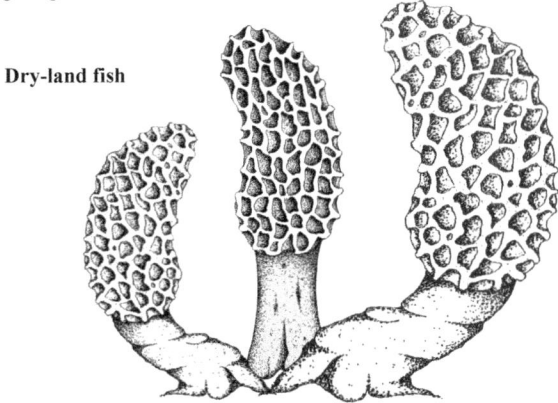

Dry-land fish

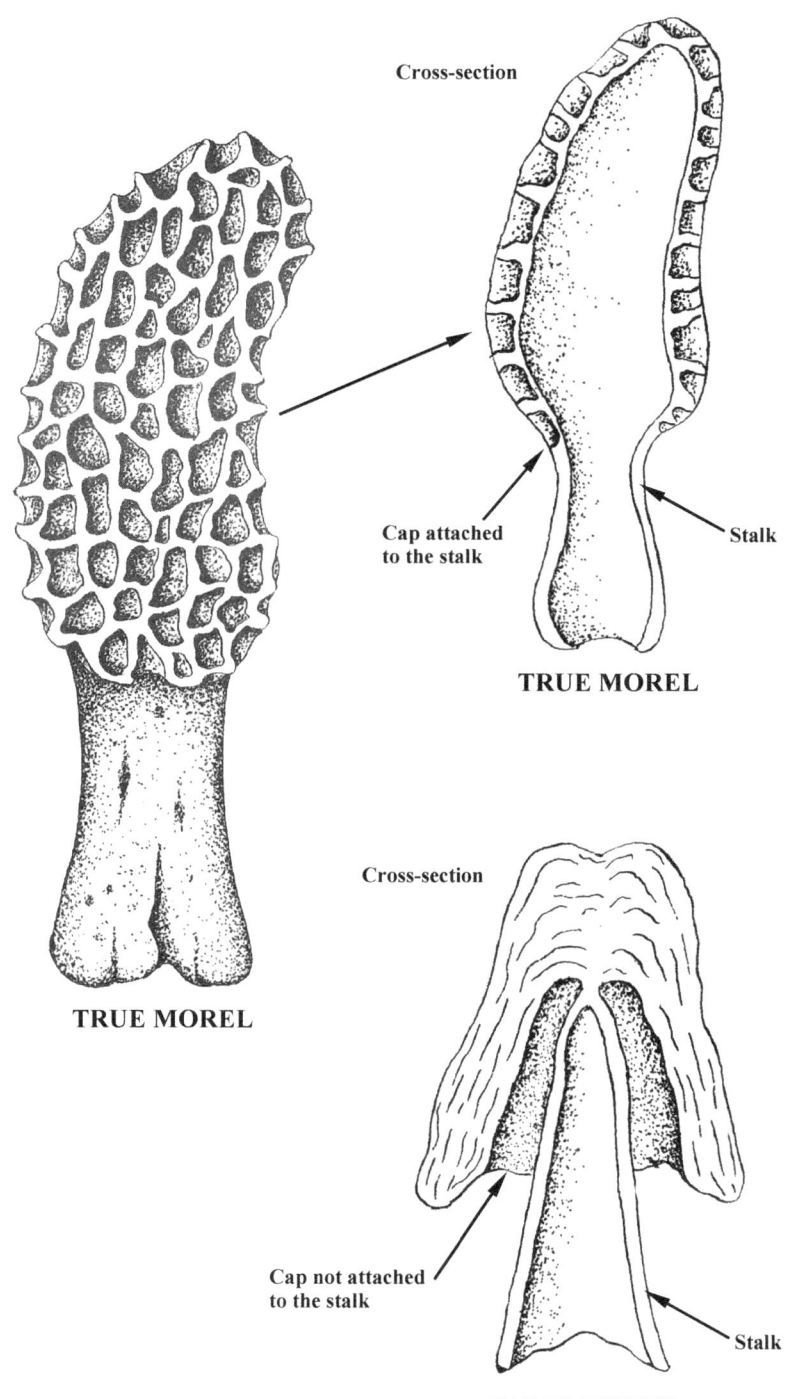

PREPARING WILD FOODS

When preparing wild foods for consumption, confirm identity of the species FIRST!

Always rinse with water to remove any debris, soil or insects.

NUTS
All nuts discussed in this book can be eaten raw or dried for future consumption. To dry nuts, first remove the outer husks, leaving the shells intact. Spread the nuts out on a flat pan and dry in a dark well-ventilated place for about a week or so. Then simply store them in a glass jar.

TEAS
Teas are usually made from the dried leaves of plants although occasionally fresh leaves are used. The drying process of leaves is simple. First collect the fresh leaves of the species and spread them out flat in a pan. Leave in a warm, shaded, well-ventilated place such as a pantry of attic for anywhere from a day to a week depending upon the humidity. When fully dry, the leaves will be crumbly. Store in an airtight container (glass works best) for future use. To make a tea, pour boiling water over the dried tea leaves and steep 5-15 minutes. Use 1 teaspoon of dried material or 2 teaspoons of fresh material for every cup of water. Strain through cheesecloth to remove any undesired material. Sweeten if desired.

GLOSSARY OF TERMS

CLEARING: An area where large amounts of sunlight can reach the ground's surface

COVE: A recessed place in the land.

DECIDUOUS: Used in reference to trees that lose their leaves in fall, such as maples and oaks

EVERGREEN: Used in reference to plants or trees that remain green all year, such as pines

FAUNA: Animal life

FLORA: Plant life

HABITAT: A plant or animal's area of existence (where they live, grow, etc.)

HOLLOW: The area that embodies a small stream or brook, a small variety

HUSK: The woody materials that are immediately covering the shells of nuts

PITHY: A spongy center of tissue in the stem of a plant

SHELL: The woody material that immediately covers the nutmeat

SPECIES: A group of individuals having common attributes

VARIEGATED: Having discrete markings of different colors

WOODED BORDER/EDGE: The area of transition between a woods and field

REFERENCES

BROCKMAN, C. F. 1968. Trees of North America. Golden Press. New York, NY

CORE, E. L & N. P. AMMONS. 1958. Woody plants in winter. The Boxwood Press. Pacific Grove, California.

FIG, D. F. 1983. Personal interview. Supervisory Resources, US Forest Service, Stanton Ranger District, Stanton, Kentucky.

HUNTER, L. J., M. C. PILKINGTON, V. M. ANDREWS, S. M. THOMAS, R. D. MOLINA, & N. L. PAIVA. 2006. Analysis of nutritional components in edible parts of eastern redbud (*Cercis canadensis* L.). Presentation at ACS conference, Houston, Texas.

MEDSGER, O. P. 1976. Edible wild plants. MacMillan Publishing Co., Inc., New York, NY.

MILLER, O. K., Jr. 1979. Mushrooms of North America. E. P. Dutton, New York, NY.

NEWCOMB, L. 1977. Newcomb's Wildflower Guide. Little, Brown, and Company, Boston, MA.

PETERSON, L. 1978. A field guide to edible wild plants of eastern and central North America. Houghton Mifflin Company, Boston, MA.

ROBINSON, J. 2013. Eating on the wide side: the missing link to optimum health. Little, Brown and Company. New York.

WHARTON, M. E. & R. W. BARBOUR. 1971. The wildflowers and ferns of Kentucky. The University Press of Kentucky, Lexington, KY.

WHARTON, M. E. & R. W. BARBOUR. 1973. Trees and shrubs of Kentucky. The University Press of Kentucky, Lexington, KY.

WONG, T. M. & E. LEROUX. 2012. Foraged flavor: finding fabulous ingredients in your backyard or farmer's market. Clarkson Potter Publishers. New York.

ABOUT THE AUTHORS

Dan Dourson is a biologist/naturalist/illustrator who has spent most of his adult life dedicated to the preservation, conservation, and understanding of the planet's more obscure animals. For nearly twenty years, Dan was a wildlife biologist for the US Forest Service, specializing in nongame management in Red River Gorge of Kentucky. In addition, he has spent more than a decade studying the land snails in the eastern United States and abroad including Belize, Guatemala, Costa Rica, Panama, and in the Amazon Basin of northwestern Peru.

Dan is the author of seven Natural History books including his first 1984 addition of *Wild Yet Tasty*, *Biodiversity of the Maya Mountains, Belize, Central America*, three field guides to the land snails of Kentucky, the Great Smoky Mountains National Park and Southern Appalachians, and West Virginia and recently completed a field guide to the land snails of Belize. He has illustrated nature books and *Wildflowers and Ferns of Kentucky, How Snakes Work,* and multiple environmental posters used in schools around Kentucky.

Judy is a retired educator who has served as Dan's field technician, research assistant, and editor for twenty-two years, as well as being his favorite wife!

Dan and Judy also managed a biological field station BFREE (Belize Foundation for Research and Environmental Education) for seven years in wild jungles of Central America.

Their family includes Austin (Samantha), Angela (Colby), and Tyler as well as seven grandchildren: Zach, Tessa, Callie, Jude, Kyle, Jackson, and Kayden.

Dan and Judy remain committed to conservation work, protecting the Earth's most amazing and underappreciated organisms. Their passion for the natural world is clearly reflected through their writing and simple lifestyle.

www.ingramcontent.com/pod-product-compliance
Lightning Source LLC
LaVergne TN
LVHW041347080426
835512LV00006B/654